NO ONIONS FOR MISS SPINACH

Chapter 1

Sunday September 3rd 1939 and Great Bɪ......... ..... - ...... with Germany. Doris and John went to Stockwell Baptist Church at 11.0 A.M. as was their usual custom on a Sunday morning. While they are in Church listening to Mr Bird's message Mr Chamberlain spoke these words.

"Now may God bless you all, May he defend the Right. It is the evil things we shall be fighting against: Brute force, bad faith, injustice, oppression and persecution and against them I am certain that the Right will prevail"

Doris lived at No 29 Bromfelde Road, Clapham with her Mother. They occupied the top flat of this three storey house. Below them lived the owners of the building, Mr and Mrs Hopgood; Two elderly but very amiable people. Living with those two were two more females by name Miss Wade and Mrs Maxxted (there is only one X that's the worst of being an amateur typist). Now these two females were relatives of the Hopgoods (They still are for that matter) They are cousins or nieces or something more or less several times removed.

Now these women differed from each other in all ways: they were as alike as chalk and cheese. The former was pleasant both in looks and temperament whilst the latter was a sour faced, bespectacled misery.

John had been living in Fentiman Road, South Lambeth ever since he first came to London to qualify as a chemist and now that he was a member of the Pharmaceutical Society he was working at Loughboro Junction, Herne Hill.

He still stayed however with the old battleaxe mainly because there was always a cup of tea to be had whatever the time of day or night and again she would always lend him a bob or two should an urgent exigency arise.

Bill Arbuckle had called for John on this particular morning very much earlier than usual as tension was running pretty high that morning and the two called at 29 Bromfelde Road to take Doris to church.

Although the sun shone in a cloudless sky yet there was an unmistakable but invisible cloud hanging over all. It brought a feeling of uncertainty with it.

In these circumstances Doris, Bill and John went to church on that never to be forgotten morning.

The last hymn had started and the congregation had sung one verse when the Church was filled with another sound, a sound which every one is familiar with by now, the wail of the air raid sirens. The service stopped abruptly with the benediction and the whole congregation left the church to take cover.

From the peace and quiet of the few minutes previous there was now nothing but uproar. Wardens dashed about the place shouting TAKE COVER at the top of their voices, cars pulled into the kerbs with terrific screeches and the police instead of subduing the tumult seemed to add to it.

Doris and her escort made a beeline for Bromfelde Road but when they were only a hundred yards from home a very officious Air Raid Warden shooshed them into the nearest house. They found that they had been shunted into the privacy of a complete stranger's home and left to their own resources. All the time the sirens continued to wail out their message of impending trouble.

Suddenly the warbling warning stabilised its note and it became apparent that the alert was over.

Thus the Cooper family and everyone else besides had their free sample of what was to come.

Twice again the warning sounded in the London area that week but luckily no planes, guns or bombs were heard.

After that initiation into war conditions London was spared the nuisance of "Moaning Minnie" (as the sirens were later christened) for a considerable time.

Meanwhile the war proceeded and now and again scattered bits of news filtered through: some good and some not so good. Judging from the bulletins issued by the governments concerned all forces, friends and foes alike were doing exceptionally well and all three countries had practically won the war. A gent who broadcast news in English for his boss, Dr Goebbels, sunk H.M.S. Ark Royal every night regularly for a fortnight and in about a month the entire British Fleet had been so damaged that it was for all intents and purposes quite useless as a fighting force. All this tommy rot was told to the English speaking world by a bloke later to be called Lord Haw Haw. Anyway, it provided us with lots of laughs.

For weeks John went on as usual, to Loughboro Junction in the morning, over to Stockwell at night and then back home to Fentiman Road so much later at night.

Doris ended her employment with Mouldy Maxie, the Market Place miser during the first few weeks and then became a regular customer at the Brixton Exchange.

Then came Christmas 1940.

Christmas Eve was dank and dark even at 4 o'clock in the afternoon and Doris and John once again made their way towards Stockwell Baptist Church. This time however they went separately. John went first with Doris's brother in law Jack Bovington and Doris went with her sister Daisy and her Mother who also boasts the same flowery Christian name.

It was only a few minutes after her arrival when instead of being Miss Doris Jenner she became Mrs Doris Cooper. Bert Potter should have been there to give John support but the fog baffled all his efforts to find the Church and while John was saying " I will " poor old Bert was grovelling about outside wasting matches in vain.
After a short Christmas honeymoon in wild and woolly Wales, the pair returned to London to set up their home.
Spring gradually gave way to summer and summer means holiday. As holidays mean another trip to Lampeter.

Union Road, Clapham merges into Bromfelde Road at a point such that the Cooper residence is immediately facing a dairy in Union Road. This Dairy is owned by a Mr and Mrs Evans and at this shop the Coopers did their grocery shopping. The proprietors were natives of Tregaron, a small town near Lampeter and were also therefore good friends of the Coopers.

Late in July the pale and frail Mrs Evans told Doris that she intended hiring a car and was going back to Tregaron to bring her children back to London, (They had been evacuated soon after war broke out), At the same time she offered to take Doris and John with her if they would pay a fair proportion of the expenses involved. As this would be much cheaper than railway fares (Please note - G.W.R.) Doris accepted the offer and so on August the fourth at nine o'clock Mrs Evans and Mr and Mrs Cooper left London by road for Lampeter.

After a particularly fine rest and holiday they returned by rail late on Saturday night. They heard all the latest gossip and scandal from Mrs Jenner (Aliases "Frau Fumph" and "Skinny - ") consumed a spot of supper and retired. Next day in the middle of lunch (dinner to you) "Mournful Minnie" interrupted and the family retired to the air raid shelter with the beef and yorkshire in their hands.

The Hopgood family however hadn't made a start on their dinner and poor mother Maxted kept moaning throughout the alert about the possibility of her Sunday grub being burnt to a cinder in the gas oven.

Then the Blitz really got going. The Germans came more and more often sometimes by day and sometimes by night.

Bill Arbuckle had been a soldier now for some time. He had been called up and was mucking about the country in all sorts of weird place: anywhere from John O'Groats to Land's End or from Pwllheli to Putney. At this juncture he decided to follow John's lead and he too got married.

This individual is a typical cockney. Either you like him or else you don't; there is no halfway about it. He most certainly likes to air his opinions - he knows all and likes to tell all but there is not much harm in him.
He is thin and scraggy and no Clark Gable by any manner of means but he is just an ordinary decent sort of bloke. One of those people who slap you on the back with an accompanying "Wotcher old cock" Doris thinks the first operation is carried out with unnecessary violence.

His favourite author appears to be Mr Hadley Chase and I am quite convinced that he goes to bed with a picture of Miss Blandish under his pillow.

William has chosen for his spouse a young lady named Doris Smith. Her name designates her character without any added description on my part; but being a contrary sort of individual I will tell you of a few of her odd ways. She is quiet and unassuming and she is very good hearted. She lacks the exotic glamour of Miss Hedy Lamarr and the voluptuous "oomph" as possessed by Miss Ann Sheridan.

Just the same this Doris too is grand company. She is also quite capable of resurrecting a real fighting spirit and ability when occasion demands. Doris Smith will be able to handle this bloke Arbuckle alright and on August the thirty first she took on the job.

Chapter 2

By Sunday September 15th things were really getting hot and we had passed the eighty mark and still going strong. This date marked the beginning of the most exciting week (Up to date of going to press) in the lives of the Cooper family). They had six raids daily on the Sabbath, the Monday and the Tuesday and they weren't tuppenny ha'penny raids either.

The next day being a Wednesday was a half holiday from the shop and John duly knocked off at one o'clock sharp and took his 34 tram to Clapham. Of course there was an air raid on at the time but that was natural enough in those days, Having found the family religiously taking cover in their shelter, he joined them until the gallant luftwaffe was fed up of dropping bombs on London.

After the raid they had a spot of dinner and then toddled off to the Brixton Astoria to keep a date with Deanna Durbin.
Our heroes (?) then prepared for their inevitable nocturnal perambulations round the backyard and true to form they came back for the hundred and second time at 8.0 P.M. sharp.

At all times Mother Maxted didn't like the shelter; she always complained of suffocation or something and always said she felt sick and makes a lot of fuss. Tonight was no exception and she said that she would stay in the kitchen until she heard anything and then trot under the stairs leading to the cellar. Miss Wade volunteered to stay with her. At eleven o'clock things started moving fast and furious - mostly in a downward direction and suddenly a terrific crash shook the shelter and the sound of breaking glass and falling masonry filled the air. The air was also filled with dust.
Mr Hopgood spoke. "Fetch those two into the shelter"
"They can't stay there with all this"

So John crossed the yard to the house to escort those women to the comparative shelter in the yard followed by well meant advice.
 "Keep the torch low" "Take care"
and still more "Be very careful"

Miss Wade said that some of our windows had gone west so John went up to the top of the building to have a quick look round. There didn't seem to be much the matter their own house. But as this is not the time for hanging about he just collected his convoy and the three trickled into the air raid shelter.

So they made their dash to the shelter and hardly had they reached cover when it happened, Without a sound of warning a second crash more ear splitting than the first rent the air, the rush of the blast soared through the house and then gradually the roar died down.

John went back to make another investigation and found that the house was very badly knocked about and it was quite apparent that anyone in the building could hardly have escaped with their lives.

Of course as it was still pitch dark it was quite impossible to assess the total damage. As all the windows had been blown out John couldn't strike a light so the only things to do was to fall over things to find out where things were. After having walked into a door lying on the floor and fallen over the hallstand which was suspended at 45 degrees across the hall, he managed to reach the front door; it wasn't necessary to open it as it had been blown down.

The sight which met his gaze told all he wanted to know; the pile of bricks and rubble the other side told the dreaded story of the final chapter in Mr and Mrs Evans's life.

He was greeted with questions like these
"Whose house was it?" "Is it very bad?" "What's happened?"
The only reply to all these questions was that the dairy wouldn't open again.
"Do you think that Mr and Mrs Evans are all right?"
"I don't see how they could possibly have escaped."

The all clear went fairly early in the morning and as it was still dark there was nothing more that could be done but stay in the shelter until there was sufficient light to see what could be done.

The house was a complete wreck so it was a case of finding somewhere to live and events moved quickly. The family were sent over to the church hall in Union Street where their names and late addresses were recorded and after having consumed a cup of tea and bun supplied by the Y.M.C.A canteen John went to Loughboro Junction to report to the boss what had occurred. After this they all went to the Magdalene Hospital at Streatham by ambulance accompanied by the hundred of others who had suffered the same misfortune.
They spent the next night here in this Rest Centre and then they were offered a billet in Balham.

And then Doris and John moved in to No. 45 Dinsmore Road. This address is the home of Alice Dick and David.
Alice is the young welsh wife of Dick a soldier in the Welsh Guards. David is their son and heir and is three years of age. Dick is stationed "somewhere in England".
David is a pretty child and very clever in many ways but his vocabulary of Billingsgate English is exceedingly large and his use of this highly coloured language is very liberal. He has the habit of speaking to total strangers and he will address these people in public places with yards and yards of abuse and invective.

This fearsome infant punctuates his sentences by spitting at the persons he speaks to. He has no respect for sex, age or honour; he spits at them all and he swears at them all. After he has annoyed anyone for a certain length of time Alice takes a hand and an active part in the proceedings. This does not have a great deal of effect as David then screams at the top of his voice and switches his abuse at his mother in even more violent vein. The whole performance has to be seen to be appreciated or even believed.

Dick now is a more sober and restrained person: one couldn't really quarrel with Dick. Darling wife Alice who is a most exasperating and effervescent female is also a a real lady when dressed up and out with hubby but you aught to see her at home. She runs about the house half dressed and shows no vestige whatever of ladyship.

Doris naturally got a trifle fed up with this sort of thing so in December an attempt was made to re-establish a home for themselves. In the meantime John still had work to do. A chemist's shop in Milkwood Road was the place where he passed his time away for his daily bread. He was employed by a chemist, Wenmoth by name and the two had worked together for some time before the war. Reggie, as his wife (Betty) very affectionately calls him, is a fat, pompous individual whose knowledge of world affairs in his own estimation is pretty complete.

His consistent pessimism is well known locally. His considered opinion of the government is that we are run by a money grabbing bunch of Jews who haven't got an ounce of brain between them.
"The dunder headed fools aught to be stuck against a wall and shot"
"They are a bunch of criminal lunatics, thieves, robbers and nitwitted twerps".

On one occasion he thought the British Empire was so decadent and the war was as good as lost when he read that the higher ups of the A.T.S. had been spending considerable time debating as to whether the girls should or should not wear red knickers with or without black spots.

His own way of running the war would get results he says. The idiots up to date have not done anything with any sense and what has been done wouldn't have been done by a sensible two year old. The only thing he doesn't say is what should be done.
His moods and opinions are governed by several factors, which although he doesn't know it, everyone he speaks to immediately recognise. These factors are mainly his wife, his selfishness and his limited outlook.

Regarding the latter he reads the "Daily Mirror" and the "Sunday Pictorial" and then swears to his customers that he never reads the papers as one cannot believe what they write. However if the report is of foreign origin it is bound to be true " - or they wouldn't say so".

Mrs Wenmoth wears the pants there is no doubt about it.
By way of example here is a short story. Mrs W came down from the house the other day and without any ado spoke to her beloved thus:-
"You haven't the brains of a maggot"

Reggie remained silent and although John was very much tempted to point out that it wouldn't have been much to his credit if he had, John too was silent. This is the way she makes him look more of a fool than he really is. And all poor Reg had done was to spill a drop of milk on the floor.

Mrs W. is selfish and jealous of those in better circumstances and Reginald has caught the disease. With him, it takes the form of mania; he had the unbreakable idea that the company shops, the Jews, the price-cutters and all the customers are determined to do him as often as possible.

And in such pleasant company John works (or pretends to).

-0-

One Friday he got there during an alert. They dropped bombs all the way up Milkwood Road and six houses collapsed under his nose so to speak; anyway within a radius of a hundred yards of the shop.

A very good friend of the Cooper's was killed during this raid. She was Phyllis Temple of Larkhall Lane. Phyl was working at Freeman's in the Clapham Road and had gone with the rest of the girls to take shelter but the bomb dropped directly on the shelter in which she waited. She was one of the kindest and sweetest girls that anyone could have wished to know and her loss came as a terrible shock to all her very any friends. The many memories that Doris and John have of Phyllis will be cherished by them all their lives.

Slowly September passed away and with it the very severe raids. They still came but not so frequently in the daytime. 18 Milkwood Road suffered at the hands of the Luftwaffe halfway through October and this meant for John a week's hard navvying, carpentering and plumbing.
Intensive shovelling was necessary to get some semblance of order out of the havoc caused.

Prepare to meet Battling Beeton, the Hearnville Horror.

At No 58 Hearnville Road, Balham there was a flat to let and Doris and Fumph bearded the owner in her den. 17/6 rent was paid immediately to take over the place and certain articles of furniture taken down from Bromfelde Road.

Mother Beeton then said that in her opinion the furniture was in such a bad condition that it would have lowered the prestige of Hearnville Road.

John then went to see the old bathbun and pointed out that although the salvaged odds and ends were not particularly elegant as they were they could easily have been renovated and then also mentioned that a landmine dropped within fifty yards of her old antiques would make them even more antiquated and useless. This remark didn't make her any better tempered so John asked her for the rent he had paid her, thanked her for her help she didn't give him, wished her good morning (mumbling something else under his breath) and cleared out. With the assistance of the billeting authorities Doris established herself at 15A Ravenswood Road. and this is where they are still in residence (even Battling Beeton has had to congratulate Doris on the good job she made of it.

During the period of storage at Streatham and Bromfelde Rd. The latter having no roof and English weather being what it is, it is not surprising that certain of the household articles had become a trifle dusty and damp to add to the damage done to the things by bomb-blast. Owing to transport difficulties and the fact that their furniture was distributed in various parts of South London it was an immense job to get all back in one place.

One particular article a wooden trunk was exceptionally difficult to corner and it was a long time before it was finally captured and brought home.

At 58 Hearnville Road there was stored a lot of furniture belonging to a relative of Mrs B. and part, if not all of it was at one time brought to Ravenswood Road with he furniture belonging to Doris. This unfortunate error was discovered and the stuff carted back. The whole lot was dumped into the sacred sanctum of the horrible horror.

When it came to pass that Mrs Beeton heard of these things she was solely vexed and great was her wrath. I am told she even gnashed her teeth but I cannot vouch for this statement. Anyhow she comes over to 15A and libels Doris very thoroughly (she made some crack about some missing spoons) I should have loved to see her tackle the removal blokes about them. She was shown the door and the matter forgotten. But not for long. John decided that the trunk had got to be fetched so he trotted round to Fontenoy Road (where lives this monstrosity) arranged with the fat old female that he intended calling for the trunk the next evening, he made a few very pointed remarks about spoons; he told her straight that statements to saying that they had borrowed them and that she was going the right way to get a basinful of trouble for herself.

14

Friday night, beside being Amami night, was the night chosen for the transfer of the trunk. At this point, we meet Ivy and Harry. This young married couple reside in Gaskarth Road up the Balham Hill. Ivy used to work with Doris at Maxie's Joint in the distant past but like Doris had given up work for the pleasure of feeding and housing a husband. Ivy is one of those fairly sensible people and makes a good hostess. She can be relied on to feed the faces of her guests with something snappy in the sandwich line and makes a real good cup of tea. (Py-shan Points naturally. Free advert) The latter capability is one of the reasons why John is fond of visiting Gaskarth Road.

When Harry sees them his invariable greeting, I nearly said War Cry meets them "Hi-yah Do-ee"   "Hi-yah Johnny"

Harry rolls his own weeds, enjoys a game of Monopoly, chess and cards and handles a nifty niblick on Clapham Common putting green. These are the two people who rallied round to the Cooper's assistance in the matter of the missing trunk. At 8'0 P.M. therefore on the appointed Friday night I. J. H. and D. strolled round to Hearnville Road. Fortunately it had been retrieved from the centre of the room where it had been embedded so it was merely a matter of humping it along the High Road homewards.

There was a noticeable resemblance to a funeral in the procession as it slowly made its way along the road in fact the local residents were not slow to exhibit their brilliant gifts of repartee and the whole thing was the subject of much comment, wit and discussion.

At Loughboro Junction there was a coffee bar owned and run by Frank and Nora. They have one little girl whose name is Gretel Ann (but who is called Chick by all and sundry). Frank has had a pretty rough time of it what with one thing and another but he has accumulated considerable experience and knowledge in a great variety of jobs, professions and hobbies. He has apparently travelled a good deal and been to most places of any importance. He can tell dozens of good yarns dealing with his various travels.

His knowledge of the culinary arts and dodges appear to be absolutely unlimited and this talent is put to good use in running a cafe in Hinton Terrace which he has acquired lately.

If you want a good dinner, a good telling off or a good argument you can't do better than visit Frank's Cafe.

Nora is always to be found with one of her cigarette holders handy; I believe she considers herself undressed if she hasn't got it. She has very definite ideas about politics and states her views in no uncertain manner. She has an extensive vocabulary and obviously has paid a lot of attention to English grammar and literature,

Number three in the Ewings family is four year old Chicko. This very attractive young lady is pretty, well spoken and also has some firm ideas on a variety of subjects (this latter almost amounts to awkwardness occasionally) but she is the apple of her Daddy's eye. She has a favourite uncle - her Uncle John.

Frank had been bombed out of his home at Dulwich, his coffee bar at the Junction and out of his shop in Flaxman Road so Nora, her mother and Chicko were sent to take up their residence at Maidenhead. Soon after this Frank took over the cafe at 5A Hinton Terrace. After a considerable time was spent gallivanting to Estate Agents he finally got things straight.

Just about this time Doris took a month's holiday and escorted her sister to John's country seat at Lampeter. Sister Daisy had had a nervous breakdown as a result of regularly sleeping down in the Underground Station at Clapham South to dodge the air raids. They left London on April 17th the day following one of London's worst raids. As London's transport system had been severely dislocated it was not surprising that they missed their train at Paddington and consequently their connection at Carmarthen. They arrived at this forsaken hole in the middle of the night and were eventually rescued by John's father who had a car sent to collect them.

Daisy is a little older than Doris and is married to a Mr Sidney Cooper. Sid is no relation to Mr John Cooper and also no relation to John's father Mr Harry Cooper; but all these Mr Coopers and Mrs Coopers the whole thing becomes a little confusing.

In the meantime John developed the habit of going to bed at an early hour. The night of May 10th passed by with a very bad raid and the following day being a Sunday John once again donned his boiler suit and turned into salvage work.
He first went to see friend Frank who told him that a landmine had been dropped on Denmark Road; so John went down the road to see if there was anything left of old Stick-in-the-mud's place.

There wasn't much.

"Stick-in-the-mud" is the pet name John has for Mr E. K Monks, Chemist & Druggist of Coldharbour Lane. John has been in the habit of doing half day duty for Mr Monks on a Wednesday for a long time and also on Sunday evenings; so to the shop went John to see what happened. Having arrived at the scene of the debacle and climbed through the wreckage into the shop he emptied the till of the loose cash and decided it was quite unnecessary to open the shop as it was wide open already.

Frank and John then donned boiler suits and returned to try to clear up some of the mess, render it fairly secure from looters and then try to contact the owner to tell him what had occurred.

Frank usually came home with John to Balham at night as Nora was still away and a more depressing place than Loughboro' is not to be found. The three usually spent the evening gassing of this and that, listening to the wireless or pursuing their latest hobby - photography. As Frank went to Maidenhead nearly every Sunday he usually had a film to develop on the Monday.

Another favourite pastime was putting on Clapham Common or on Tooting Bec. In this game Frank seemed quite unable to resist the temptation to biff the pill from one end of the green to the other. Although John would really try to take as few strokes as possible, Frank would clout the ball unnecessarily fiercely and would lose all patience with the ball if he hadn't put it in, in about three strokes. Doris gradually improved her technique and is now a reliable player. If when she is making her shot her attention isn't distracted by the sight of legs walking in the corner of her eye she can often sink a six or seven foot shot.

Table-tennis is another game at which Frank, Nora, Doris and John used to put in a lot of practice both at Frank's own place in Hinton Road and at the Lucania Club in Brixton near the Astoria Cinema. Frank has an assortment of real red hot shots but his eyes are not what they used to be so he is in fact rather handicapped. Ping-pong the like of which has never been seen has been played at Frank's Cafe. The male part of the quartet has developed a "hit anything anywhere anyhow" policy.

Regarding that more sober amusement chess, John has several opponents and passes hour after hour with one or another of them.

Rival number one is Reggie, the boss. Now this gent plays a very careful and guarded game and rarely makes a daft move so John has to bring to bear all the cunning at his command. It is a case of the strategy born of years of experience versus the strategy of youth.

Frank Ewings the head cook and bottle washer of 5A Hinton Terrace and John's closest collaborator and associate has a somewhat terrifying method of play. His policy appears to be to bring all his major pieces up quickly and sail through his opponent's defence without the slightest regard for loss. He is quite capable of sacrificing any number of his men to disrupt his enemy's plans.

Blitzkrieg in the real sense. Adolf has a lot to learn from Frankie. This type of play is adequately suited to the conditions under which the two have to play.

Usually the programme of the dinner hour runs something like this.
1.0 - 1.5 P.M. .... Arrive for dinner
1.10 .... Start dinner
1.25 .... Set up chess board

1.30 .... Frank sits down
1.31 .... Frank gets up again
1.32 .... Frank sits down, lights a fag, swallows a mouthful of tea and moves his King's Pawn up.

1.33 .... John does the same move and the game proceeds until a customer gets up and speaks. "Two o' drip please mate"

1.34 .... Two o' drip fetched for man

1.35 .... Game restarted. Several moves may be made until the next interruption.

1.37 .... "Give us a slice of bread and ten weights, will you?"

1.45 .... The game proceeds along its somewhat erratic course   by kind permission of the boys.

Expressions of surprise, indignation and amusement accompany the game.

The following weird conversation emanated from the end table the other day.

"Got your full complement?2
"No, I am a pawn and a horse short"
"There's a horse behind the mustard pot"
"Lets get cracking"
"Who's blitz?"
"Yours"
"Right"
"You can't put that blinking thing there"
"Why not?"
"You're on check"
"What from?"
"My august queen"
"Lumme, it looks as if I've got to shift the regal peanut"

John's next opponent is Doris. Doris however has only recently learnt the moves and a lot of bribery and corruption is needed to induce her to play at all.
Harry also has just been initiated into the realms of chess strategy but he certainly takes a very intelligent interest in the game and I am certain that with a bit of practice he would become a mighty stiff opponent to come up against. However that may be but if you suggest a game of Monopoly to Harry you will find that's right up his street so to speak.

Harry has some curious ideas about big business but they are all quite sound ones. He never possesses two halfpennies (In the game of Monopoly) for a penny.

He invests all the lot, lock, stock and barrel. He always develops his property up to the hilt so it's look out when you alight on it. Ivy on the other hand always tries to collar all the property going and so she is collecting small amounts of money all the way around the board and Harry's collections are few and far between but you do really get stung if you are sitting pretty on it.

Chapter 3

One of the best things in life is to see Doris behind the counter of a chemist's shop. Once a week Doris and John make tracks for Camberwell Green where at the shop belonging to Mr Monks they do half day duty. (Mr Monk's Pharmacy has long since been made habitable after the bump it had in May) Doris really takes an honest interest in the customers but she somehow goes too far (in my opinion anyway). She seems to think that the customer is always right. This is a fallacy which ought to be exploded once and for all: the customer is never right unless you happen to be a customer. Doris doesn't seem to realise that people who think they are ill on half days or late at night are merely selfish idiots who ought to be put away.

Patients should only be ill at convenient and respectable hours and not when their doctor and chemist want their hard earned game of golf. Such is life; and it is to these thoughtless individuals that John and Doris gave up their half holiday without the slightest regard for the 2/6 financial gain.

The pair usually arrive in the vicinity of 5.00 P.M. count the money in the till if any and then look around to see if there is anything worth selling in the shop. (They don't forget to look under the counter as well as on top of it). Just to illustrate what sort of sales-lady Doris is let me tell you a story...

John has just acquired a set of artificial teeth and one day told Doris that he was considering getting either a tin of Steradent or a tin of Milton Denture Powder for the purpose of cleaning them. (Please note; I do not get any fee whatever for these free adverts.) Doris however ups and says "You needn't bother, I have a tin of Harpic in the scullery"

In the event of your not knowing what this commodity is I will inform you later on. As there is sometimes a spot of dispensing to do and the patients don't come in till late, it annoys John a good deal. He says he cannot imagine why they are called patients: he hasn't met one yet who is. They may be at the doctor's surgery but they certainly aren't at the chemist's dispensary; you would think they hadn't a minute to live, some of them.

Dispensing is certainly a weird and wonderful business. At nine o'clock in the morning (in theory anyway) John arrives at No 18 and disappears into a world of Trychloro-phenylmethyl-iodo-salicylp-Sulphonilimide Phosphotungstic Acid and Aspirin. There he stays surrounded by bottles of solids and liquids, powders and crystals and dozens of other mysterious and evil-smelling drugs.

Curious slips of paper are handed in to him all day on which are written the weirdest hieroglyphics. John then grabs a bottle, adds to the contents of one bottle a portion of something from another, mixes the lot together, fills up the first bottle with something out of a tap and low and behold; a cough cure or medicine for tummy ache just like that. This bottle is then labelled "three times a day", the prospective corpse's name added and there you are.

Of course John doesn't receive his salary merely for his pharmaceutical activities at the shop, he has to talk a lot of rot about Bile Beans, Kruschen Salts,
in-growing toenails and spotted earache. Mrs W. is also quite likely to want a loaf of bread, a bucket of coal or a spot of loose change. Again it may be necessary to give a hand in a first class brawl with one of the Wenmoth's tenants. The hedge of the flat might want clipping, the electric light might have fused, the water mains might have burst or the sewers might be stopped up. If a customer wants a cat mercifully popped off, the first question is "Where is Mr Cooper?" Sign writing, plumbing and carpentering all come into the daily routine. Such is a part of the working day of Reggie's factotum (otherwise the boss's stooge).

P.S. Harpic is primarily intended for cleaning lavatory pans...

Chapter 4

For some time now there is a little job which must be done by all those mere males who haven't the intelligence to think up ways of avoiding it. Fire watching.

Here again we find the Coopers well in the middle of it. Doris is only an amateur fire-spotter and hasn't been in the business very long but she has already acquired a fully trained status. John on the other hand is an old stager, a professional 3/- a time and qualified fireguard.

He has not received any practical work on the subject and has never (up to date) seen an incendiary bomb in action. Doris does firewatching on Monday nights in Ravenswood Road and although she has not been a member for a month she has been yanked out of bed at the disgraceful hour of 3.00 A.M. to keep her peepers open for firebombs. John does firespotting on two fronts. Firstly at Milkwood Road one night in every eight and secondly at home with Doris on Monday nights.

At Milkwood Road, John doesn't officially start until ten o'clock or so and after a few games of chess with Reginald the pair prepare for the night. Reggie takes his place on a mattress and John dosses and dozes on a deckchair up in the sitting room. Providing the night passes quietly (it usually does) John rises at 6 o'clock, makes a cup of tea, eats a couple of meat-paste sandwiches carefully prepared by the Missus, calls Reggie and then knocks off. The first thing he then does is to call on Frank to see if there was anything doing during the night that he might have slept through.

The Ravenswood Road affair is quite voluntary and both Doris and John felt anxious to co-operate in any reasonable scheme to prevent the fire habits of the Luftwaffe getting them anywhere. On the appointed night therefore they retire to bed with all their equipment near and with their "north ear" open for any signs of aerial activity.

Chapter 5

During the past two months there has been a new occupation to claim the attention of the inmates of 15A. They are now busily engaged in "Digging For Victory". The credit for the idea goes to Frank and Nora as indeed does the credit for the good work. So the four gardeners took up the job of cultivating the land which was the site of two large houses in Barrington Road before they received the attention of Adolf's flying fools. After having removed what remained of the houses in question they found the "good earth" and then waded in to dig it up. Potatoes, onions, beetroot and all the usual vegetable grown by amateur gardeners took their place. During sundry scrounging visits to bombed premises, sufficient wood was obtained to build a reasonable likeness to a shed. We also will find a swing there on which Chicko indulges in hair-raising feats. "Waltzing Matilda" is the truck which was designed and built for the express purpose of transporting H2O to the garden.

At seven, John leaves the shop and walks down the road to find Frank has already done a couple of hours down on the farm and has returned with "Waltzing Matilda" who is then parked outside 15A. After having filled up a couple of baths with water they make their perilous trip to the garden. Halfway there it is necessary to cross the tram track. The track here carries the notorious No 34 service and at this point does no credit to those people who lay tram tracks; a more bumpy section of line is not to be found. All this would be very irrelevant to gardening if it weren't for the fact our gardeners have to negotiate this tram line in the course of their trip with their load of water to the garden. They consider themselves extremely fortunate if they arrive at their destination with 75% of the water that they started with.

The garden however turned out to be extremely successful and is certainly a credit to those who did so much work on it.

No chronicles of the gardening activities would be complete without the story of the Gherkin. They thought it would be a good idea to grow a couple of gherkin plants in an odd corner of the garden so when all the really urgent work was more or less completed Nora trotted down to a small shop called Woolworths and bought a couple of small gherkin plants. These were taken to the garden with due fuss and ceremony. They were planted in a special bed made to receive them but one, sad to relate, died.

The plant left however continued to thrive and grew and grew. It was covered with glass, manicured carefully and watered conscientiously. It was diligently watched and taken care of. The gherkin continued to thrive and soon filled the bed.

It still grew and grew and grew into one of the finest thistles that you have clapped eyes on.

Chapter 6

One of the most frequent visitors at the Cooper homestead is Doris's sister Grace, usually accompanied with daughter Patricia and occasionally with hubbie Jack.

Jack if you remember was John's aide-de-camp at his wedding and now spends his time gallivanting around the countryside on war work of no importance in the engineering line. Grace impedes the war effort by chasing him around. Jack goes someplace and finds digs for Grace and Pat who dash after him. Then Jack moves somewhere else.

The process is then repeated and I suppose will continue to be repeated until the war finishes. Between times they look in at Balham. Bedlam reigns in Balham. I am firmly convinced that two-year-old Pat has more clothes than Doris, John and dear old Fumph put together. In every place imaginable, chairs, shelves and table you will find them.

Pat doesn't ever seem to want to go to bed at night and doesn't want to stay in bed in the morning. A most astonishing child. She also has peculiar habits with animals.

At Doris's home there are a cat (Moggy) and two recent additions as yet unnamed and these animals are subjected to the most peculiar form of affection that I have ever come across. Young Pat will pick them up by whichever appendage is nearest, stroke them with quite unnecessary gusto and then drop them into their box. She seems to delight in half strangling them (not of course from any evil intent but she just seems to think that they are made of cast iron or something). She has just reached that stage in life when walking is a sort of staggering waddle from side to side. If an animal was a cross between a duck and a lobster and in an inebriated condition much the similar style in locomotion would result. She must have a very highly developed sense of humour as you usually see her with a grin on her face from ear to ear for no apparent reason.

Jack is an individual who can throw a nifty double twenty (comes of much practice), who has no teeth (of his own) and has a very gruff voice (presumably the result of making himself heard above the din of pneumatic drills).

Having had a slight insight into the private lives of John and Doris, their relatives and their friends, we can turn our attention to the domestic surroundings in which they live. 15A Ravenswood Road is situated strange as it may seem in a road called Ravenswood. It is in the S.W.12 district of London. It is a side street off the Balham High Road, down at the bottom of Balham Hill. If you are walking from Clapham Common in the direction of Tooting you will pass the underground station at Clapham South and further along on the right, the Odeon Cinema.

Continue down the hill and you will pass a very dilapidated theatre known as the Hippodrome. The Happydrome as it is now known has been closed for a long time and has been like dozens of other big buildings knocked about by enemy action.

Passing the Happydrome the next building which serves as a landmark is the Congress Hall on the right. This is the meeting place of the local Salvation Army and here you will find the Army lassies banging their tambourines in the early years.
This hall is a favourite haunt of Mrs Jenner (Doris's mother). Opposite this meeting place is the illustrious Ravenswood Road.

Having knocked on the door of NO 15A and obtained admission you are confronted by one of the inmates and a picture of several cows. Depending on whether or not you have wiped your feet on the mat carefully and thoughtfully supplied for the purpose you will be invited into the sitting room or into the kitchen.

Presuming that you have, you are then shown into the first door on the right. The dominating feature of this room is the Blitz Bed which has been painted a brilliant green. The room has been tastefully furnished in a modern style. One picture only hangs on the walls; a futurist drawing representing "Creation" copied from a small sketch which was published in a radio newspaper. The drawing drew John's attention as soon as he saw it and he wasn't satisfied until he had made a very much larger copy.

In one corner there is a bamboo bookcase filled with a varied selection of books and magazines. There are books about medicine and books about murder; magazines of love and magazines about learning. John owns a comprehensive selection of Lilliputs, London Opinions and kindred publications in which are the finest collections of photographs of the loveliest ladies you could wish to see. Near the fireplace there is a small table which Doris and John "knocked up" one day when they had nothing better to do.

Passing through the corridor we meet the lady of the house in her private sanctum. And here at this centre of industry we find the pilot at the helm.

Here the pair plan their plots and plot their plans, this is the place where John shoves his feet up on the mantelpiece and relaxes.

Chapter 7

At this stage we must turn our attention to wireless. Radio reception has become one of the chief delights of the Cooper household. Some time ago they acquired a small battery set of uncertain origin but as a battery set did not turn out to be so successful, John with Frank's assistance got hold of an A.C. Mains unit and thus converted it into a semi-mains set. Now it works usually very well and has provided hours of entertainment.

Occasionally it gets a fit and throws a temperament. On these occasions it flatly refuses to go at all. One day recently the set developed one of its fits and all
attempts by both John and Doris to coax one little squeak out of it were in vain.
John decided to take the Mains Unit to bits and this was done; they found a loose wire but they couldn't find where it had come from so they had to get the wireless man to put that right. When this had been done, the set should have gone but still she was as dead as a doorknob.

Eventually Uncle David came over, looked at the set, stuck his stethoscope all round it and then diagnosed the trouble - the fuse had blown. In the ordinary way this would have been the first thing that they would have looked at but they had neglected that this time and had practically dismembered the thing before passing it on to expert hands.

Of course this wireless set is not the first one that they have had. John spent the colossal sum of 2/6 on two separate occasions on two sets both of which worked well in pre-blitz days. The remains of one is still to be found in the Cooper homestead although it is in an almost indecent state. The home of this mechanical relic is John's office. This office in actual fact is a converted pantry and is cluttered up with the most appalling collection of junk imaginable.

At first glance it looks like a cross between a rag and bone shop and an extremely untidy village post office-grocery-ironmonger's store. There are two wide shelves running around two walls on which can be found half a dozen cameras, stacks of boxes, a large collection of various wireless components and electrical accessories of all kinds. Apart from these there are drawing instruments, pens, pencils and rolls of drawing paper and once again we find magazines by the hundred.

Even in this comparatively large space there is insufficient room for an "Alta" vertical enlarger which John has to park away from his other photographic equipment, in the alcove. If you happen to want anything from a photograph of May West to a small spanner you can get it from the "office". Photography has at one time and another been one of the favourite hobbies of Doris and John. Although operations in this line have been considerably curtailed during the war they still sometimes drag out the dishes and chemicals and do a bit of printing or enlarging.

Doris seems to enjoy making things. If it isn't a frock for Pat or Mrs Webb's baby (which ahs only just arrived anyway) she is sewing up some new curtains, a cover for her dressing table or a new set of smalls. She was continually knitting at one time but the tide of enthusiasm appears to be receding at the moment. She always appears to have half finished garments about the place which bear no resemblance whatsoever to what they are intended to be but gradually order takes the place of the chaos and lo and behold out of that ancient old hat that Aunty Amy gave her five years ago she has a perfectly dinky tea-cosy.
"It's marvellous isn't it?" I cannot tell you of all the things she has made.   I know what she would say and I suppose all her friends
        "You are so divinely wude!"

Expression picked up from a book and adapted for common use on any relevant occasion.

Chapter 8

The war has brought to the Cooper family lots of new jobs, not one of the least of which is the filling up of forms. I do well realise that most other people are affected in a similar way but I do think that the Cooper family have had a rather bad attack of the disease.

In the first case when they had been bombed out they had to fill up forms at the Church Hall, Magdalene Hospital and at Wandsworth Town Hall. They had to fill in forms to get their furniture to storage and more to get it out again. Forms to go into their billet and forms to leave it. Forms to fill in for this that and the other. Being a trifle short of cash to replace immediately their essential furniture they filled up forms at the U.A.B. and got £10, filled up forms at the Town Hall and got some furniture. The they (Town Hall) got the idea that their claims which they filled up between times had been paid off and then asked for the return of furniture loaned. This idea had to be contradicted and more forms had to be filled in to keep the furniture.

Doris registered for National service while she was in Lampeter with her sister. Tooting Ministry then wanted to know why she hadn't registered. They had by all accounts never heard of Lampeter. She sent up forms in explanation and has had three interviews but nothing else.

John gets six months reservation at a time and has to fill up forms for the Central Pharmaceutical War Committee and the Ministry of Labour. A questionnaire which asks more questions than have ever been put to the Brains Trust has to be filled up by the employer and employee and which requires a a brains trust to understand let alone fill up.

Fire watching provides another endless source of forms. As John was about six months late applying for subsistence allowance he had a stack of paper to complete, two for each night in which he had done firewatching. This form B has now to be filled up regularly every 28 days. Each time he send in a claim a warden comes round bringing reams of forms and literature for him to wade through (they must think he is the local salvage collector). There is I.C.E. 4/93 dealing with "liaison with Industrial and Commercial Concerns" and H.S.C 98/42 "The Business Premises Order" among the latest bunch of literature.

John usually goes to the Lambeth Town Hall with form B himself and at the same time tries to sort out some of the other Official Rules at the same time. From time to time he has to chase forms and notices all around the Town Hall. During his perambulations he meets dozens of assorted females in the various departments. There are young girls and aged spinsters; blondes and brunettes; tall and short but whatever their pattern they are always doing one of three things - making tea, drinking it or calling up their boyfriends on the telephone. Of course there are times when they do a little work but these are as few and far between as duck's teeth.

Conversation between John and member of Town Hall staff:-

J. "Can the Ministry of food give me a permit for Olive oil or Nut oil?"

S. "You must apply to the Oils & Fats Dept"

J. "Where do they live?"

S. "Vincent House, Vincent Square"

J. "Will they take a phone call?"

S. "No, you must send a card"

J. "Who do I see about our sugar allowance?"

S. "That lady in brown"

J. to Y.L. in B. "Can you increase our sugar allowance?"

Y.L. in B. " I am afraid you will have to state your case in writing to the food office's   Executive Officer"

J. "Is the gent in at present?"

Y.L. in B. "No"

J. "I thought not"

J. "Well look, where can I get a list of foods which are price controlled?"

Y.L. in B. "At H.M. Stat. Office in Kingsway"

J. "Thank you very much"

and so it goes on. hundreds of questions on a hundred articles and topics.

Coal rationing
Coal registration
Coke   ditto
Soft soap, liquid soap and soft oils.

And in this maze of questions you are surrounded by maddened crowds of hysterical women bawling and screaming for attention.

The staff do not appear to improve the good humour of these females as they perform with amazing slowness and appear to have not the slightest interest in their clients.

Over in the corner you may see a fat woman yelling at a ginger headed clerk that she must have more milk for her Maggie.
Another equally evil and fat female wants to change her butcher on the grounds that he never has any offal. Some have lost their identity cards, their pink points or their yellow supplement: they have all however lost their tempers.

What a life!

....

Second thoughts.

All this rubbish was written at Balham during 1942 and then typed by the author while on holiday in Lampeter. The paper on which it was printed was originally the property of Mr Harry Cooper, father of the author.

It is irrelevant to state that permission was not asked or granted for the use of either but nevertheless thanks are tendered.

Mr Harry Cooper is the "Big chief" at the local station. He is also the secretary and (over) active playing member of Lampeter Bowling Club.

Apart from this particular vice, he is pretty well harmless. He has never taken to drink, drugs, wife-beating and up to the moment hasn't spent much time as one of His Majesty's guests. Of course we realise he may possibly have to face a murder trial (for murdering his son after having read this).

Mother Cooper referred to affectionately as "Little Amy" is addicted to "First Aid to the Injured" as well as to Daddy, Kitty and her son. Where you find Mother you will find an assortment of Cats. Mrs Cooper and Cats are synonymous terms. Kitty Cooper now the local stooge of the G.P.O. is trying to find out what inductance really is. Emrys has a word for it but she doesn't believe all she hears. Kitty ("Man's Job") Cooper used to sell panties at Rhys Hughes for a few shillings a week but is now serving her country at war work for a little more.

Eileen (evacuated) Daly comes from a small place called Liverpool, completes the Cooper household at Lampeter.

To be continued (perhaps) ...

"Doris" by Doé

(with notes from Christine)

*Richard S. (my biological father) left my mother £20 when he died, one room rent free until we (the children) went to work.
      (*Mum told me his name was Smith*)

She treasured the 1/4 lb tea that his sister Lou gave her after the funeral as when alive he used to dish it out on a saucer, likewise the jam. He thought that my mum drank too much tea. He had money but bought the cheapest of everything. Daisy used to go shopping with him once a week to the Home & Colonial grocers shop in Stockwell.

My mother was born in Camberwell, Lomond Grove. She was born on July 19th 1883.
She had two sisters Amy & Flo & three brothers Harry, Arthur and Ernie (They were all older). The site where they lived now has a grand building, the Southwark Crown Court, on it.

They didn't have a lot of money as the dad became a heavy drinker & the mother coped by pawning the boy's suits. I don't know about when they were really young but I know that my mum attended the Salvation Army and so she didn't like it when she was asked to go to the pub with a jug and get it filled with ale. She was totally against drink.

Mum couldn't read or write, owing to the fact that she was constantly not well and left school at twelve. She could just about sign her name for her pension. I always wondered why I didn't try and teach her. The story goes that her father went out one day and met a man preaching on the corner of a street with a proper reading desk in front of him. This man took her father home and converted him, he told her father that he had just lost his wife & had two boys, David & Richard & no-one to help, so her father said that he would send his daughter Daisy to look after him and the boys. Mum liked the younger boy, David (but he died from peritonitis). The other boy was a teenager who objected to my mother. A few years passed and my mother had become like a wife to Richard (senior) but he didn't marry her; she was about twenty four and he was in his fifties & she had a baby, Lily.

My Aunty Amy and Arthur Sparrow, her husband, said they would like to raise the baby as their own as they couldn't have children. One day, my mum went to visit and little Lily was sitting on the step while they were in the pub so she took her home but that night they were banging on the door demanding the baby back.

The next three years went by & mum had Daisy and then after four more years, she had Grace and four more passed and she had me, Doris. She named us all after the sisters at her church.
I remember her laughing one day, nearly choking, when Daisy said "I've just seen your fat sister Doris"

Mum was a very nervous person and seemed frightened by everybody. She fainted nearly every Sunday at church and was carried out & given smelling salts)

(The sermon must have been pretty much & powerful "hell and brimstone"!).

I used to be walking behind wondering what it was all about. No wonder I grew up in fear of things.

When Richard, the eldest son, got married, he bought his wife (who had TB) to the house, it wasn't really a house as it had two shops and we entered through the glass front door with Richard's (the father) name on it. He had been a carpenter, *upholsterer and a funeral director. Anyway getting back to Richard Jnr. bringing his wife and two children home; He put his father in one room at the top of the building and us three in the other top room.

We had no gas, electric or anything. Mum cooked on the bedroom fire and we lit an oil lamp at night.

(I think Daisy must have gone to live with her employer at this stage).

When Richard died, he was eighty eight years old and I was six.

(Her father was an upholsterer and would have been contemporary with William Morris at Merton. Which may go some way to explain her extraordinary interest and knowledge of
Morris and the Pre-Raphaelite movement)

The Salvation Army gave mum a fortnight's holiday in Tankerton.

(Tankerton was where sister Daisy was to retire to many years later).

We stayed at the Annie Wilson House , they let her take me as well as I was so young. It was a lovely holiday but being fussy about my food & didn't like the tapioca pudding so mum ate two helpings. She wasn't happy as some of the women there went to the pub & accused her of staying in the house to get "favours" (like more to eat). Being Salvation Army they shouldn't have been drinking anyway.

Neighbours back home were kind and made me dresses & got me a panama hat. I always seemed to have tidy clothes but lived in plimsolls & sandals for shoes.

The two shops downstairs: one a tailor and the other a shoe mender (Mr Bootie).

The tailor was a Mr Rowe and his son had a stocking shop & stall in Brixton (Electric Avenue) and they gave Daisy a job and asked her to go and live with them as Harry Rowe went away a lot and his wife & two children liked her. They had a nice home and was made welcome, she was fourteen.

Grace and myself used to attend Sunday School at Studley Road Methodist Church & later on went to the church. They had a girls' club there, we used to have drill & concerts there. Grace won all the prizes; best all round girl, most popular girl, best at marching... I thought I was good but never won anything.

I took part in the pantomimes Cinderella and Beauty & the Beast; I was a fairy in another with wings on the dress. As an elf when very small & the story goes that I was splitting out of my costume.

After Mr Rowe (the tailor) we had Mr Winter in the shop. He was like an uncle to Grace and me, he cooked her chips and corned beef but I wouldn't eat any. He paid the 1/6 for me to go to a dancing club at Brixton (Ivy Leaf

Club for old soldiers) I like the ballet and singing but mum got turned out for laughing: we were all jogging up & down with our hands on each others hips and the kid behind was pulling my pants down.
The lady who ran it was a Miss Doris Walters who had a professional act with another lady called Gert & Doris. John and I saw them once at the Brixton Empress (we went there quite often). I often wondered if Miss Walters was the sister of *Jack Warner'   *("evenin' all").
A lot of theatrical people lived or lodged in Brixton.

Mum used to get two girls to see me over the busy Brixton Road. A long walk for a seven year old, I walked around the back of the Astoria, down Stockwell Road, then across to the underground station, down Binfield Road to Larkhall Lane.
I can still walk for miles but not uphill.)

The wanted me to go to Blackpool in pantomime singing "bring a smile to old Broadway". I learned all the words but my mum wouldn't let me go. So that was the end of my stardom.

Daisy went to the Astoria on one occasion and encouraged by her friend she entered a competition to speak a few lines and have her picture taken. Lo and behold she won.

She was a bit of a stunner in those days (although she wasn't so bad in later years). Following the competition she had to go to Elstree for a film test but she came 2nd, losing to a more professional person but it was an exciting experience for her.

Lily and Daisy went to a dance together one night at the Brixton (Ivy Leaf Club again) and they met Sid Cooper (*Daisy's future husband*) who offered to take them home. He asked how it was if they were sisters one lived in Camberwell and the other in Trelawn Road, Brixton. They explained that Lily lived with her aunt and Daisy with her boss.

Anyway Daisy made a date with him but didn't turn up. As he had had a few drinks, she didn't think he would remember and years later she remembered that he had gone looking for her in the pouring rain and he said that he never said anything that he didn't mean. Sid was like that all his life.

Daisy did get engaged before Sid to an Eddy Dobson but he was a two timer and when she met Sid she gave Eddy his ring back.
The story goes that he was a prisoner of war and his mother told Daisy that losing her to Sid was the worst thing that happened to him.

We didn't see a lot of Lily but I was given a penny every Wednesday to go from school on a 34 tram to Camberwell to see my Aunt & my mum would already be there. Aunt cooked for us but I wouldn't eat the meal.
At Xmas we would visit and in them days I didn't mind sausages (wouldn't eat them today) so while they ate turkey, I had sausages.
I made a nice friend in the buildings my aunt lived in (Peabody Buildings) - they were given to the men who were injured in the first world war and after our one room, I thought it was a palace & I would play with Stella Ashby in the square outside.

Home at 69 Larkhall Lane in the one room we had when Richard S died was lit by a paraffin lamp and was not very comfortable. We were infested with bed bugs & mum had to put paraffin around the iron bedstead legs to deter them. It was very disturbing.

Lily used to do all her own ironing and used to throw hankies at me that she didn't want; I didn't know that they were what the kids had dropped at the school where Uncle Harry was a helper to the caretaker. She used to come and visit us at xmas with my present, usually a doll all dressed up in knitted clothes my aunt had made. Grace would take me to the pantomime every year after xmas at Brixton, we would line up for hours for sixpence in the Gods. One year she cut my hair first with a pudding bowl over my head, I looked a sight. No wonder I don't like the hairdresser's now but I loved the pantomime and still do.

I went to the pictures at Brixton a few weeks ago and they have refurbished it. The young man said that one of the new parts (three cinemas in one) was the old theatre that I had gone to.

Memories of Larkhall Lane when I was 11 or 12 years old

I used to help at Nash's Laundry a few doors up, I helped Ada pack the clean clothes and sort out the stiff collars which were worn by men at the time. For my efforts, I got a shilling on a Saturday and tips for taking the laundry home to customers. I was given cocoa and buns for a mid-morning treat.

The corn chandler at the corner of Jeffries Road was a mean man who never parted with his pennies. I would playfully take a peanut out of his sack of parrot food and run out of the shop with him in hot pursuit.

My best friend was Jessie West whose mum and dad ran the greengrocer's shop next door. He took us both to Covent Garden early in the morning in his horse and cart and return home with all the fruit and veg he had got for the day.

In the summer school holidays, we usually got a month, Jessie and I and friends played in the street: Hopscotch, spinning tops and skipping and ball games. We'd also go to parks & commons, always walking to them: Kennington, Vauxhall and Brockwell parks. Clapham Common was our favourite. Grace swam out in one of the ponds and someone saved her from drowning.

She became a good swimmer and could dive off the top board at the swimming baths. She put Daisy and myself off swimming by letting go of Daisy and putting me in the deep end, just because she had no fears of water.

When I was about 14 my aunty lent, or got on the never never, a gramophone. I think she paid sixpence a week, it was wonderful, we got records from woolly's, tunes like "Love in bloom" "Lets fall in love". Daisy and Grace used to buy song sheets with all the words and we'd sing along.

Daisy's favourite tune was "If I had a Million Dollars".

She went to the Girls' Brigade at Stockwell Baptist (where I got married) and won prizes for reciting her favourite which was so long. Barbara Frietchie by Whittier.

"Up from the meadows,
Rich with Corn
Cool on a September morn..."

We couldn't bear to hear it, it drove us mad and we would say "Oh, not again".

She won an inkwell in the shape of a fireman's helmet and she used to ask "what happened to my inkwell?"

I was born in Larkhall Lane, Clapham but after seventeen years, we were left just the one room, so my mother got a flat with two rooms in Bromfelde Road with a black cooker on the landing, we loved it as we hadn't had a cooker before, mum had cooked on an open coal fire with coal she had to carry home. To this day, I am a vegetarian as I couldn't stand stews or soggy puddings.

We weren't allowed to use the bath so Grace and I used to go to the Manor Street Baths and we got told off for singing too loud. No wonder I was so happy when I got the flat with a bathroom.

I think when mum moved from Larkhall Lane to Bromfelde Road, she must have left a load of stuff behind. Mum had a box that the old man had made and a blind friend had made these rollers with slits that played "The Dead March" etc
I don't know what happened to that but it would have been a museum piece by now.
(I don't know but I think these rollers were the ones that when inserted into an automatic piano played tunes - I saw one once in a house opposite 15a)

Talking of the old man, apparently he had a horse & van contraption that he used for arranging the funerals. The horse would go through the glass front doors, down a plank of wood into a shed. Mum and he also used to take work home on a barrow. I found a picture in a book of the same two things and what looks like him sitting on top of the contraption in a funny top hat.

My Uncle Arthur who Lily lived with was a compositor at the Co-op Printing Society, Blackfriars so Lily went to work there when she left school and became a finisher. In those days, they folded the print with a bone and in later years when I helped a friend with printing, she used to say "I could do that".

The friend that I helped was Geoffrey Shroubsall. When we came to Ravenswood Road, we joined a political party and Geoffrey took us to all his functions (he was a councillor).

We went to dinners for the Rotary Club Masonic Lady's nights and the Mansion House when he became Mayor of Wandsworth.

He had a battery factory (GNU) at the end of Ravenswood Road and we all became friends. Our front room became the committee rooms during elections.

After a good many years, he had two fires at the factory that finished him (*business wise*) but a local builder gave him a workshop and I helped him do some printing. The bank loaned him money to buy a variprinter which let you insert type fonts. He became very good at the artwork but people started asking for tools for the battery trade and so we made all sorts of things and for twenty years, I worked like a Trojan until it got too much for him and he collapsed behind the printing machine. I called the ambulance but he died the following day.

At the moment its feeling sad as I have lost all my three sisters, my mum and my son that I had ten years after Christine. He died this year after Xmas 1995.

I looked after him for about a year, had nurses & helpers as he couldn't walk. He was also given an electric bed that went whichever way you wanted.

He had lived in Wales with Sue and her three children, they were soul mates and she was very upset when she found it was too much for her and he came home.

He had had a good life although he was only 38. He had belonged to a Siddha Yoga group and been all around to places like India, Switzerland and America. He also lived in an Ashram for a year. At the clinic where John died, I met a lady who was an ex-actress, Joyce Grant who did voluntary work there and we became friends. She knew all the actors and told me stories of them. Nigel Hawthorne was one of her friends and he signed and sent me a book. Joyce is going to South Africa for five months and will return in June 1996.

After Leaving school

I went to Priory Grove School and left there at 14 years old and got a job at Valentine & Norris in the Wandsworth Road. The had about six shops in a row. At first I was in the shop that sold vests and pants or in the hat department.

I also helped to take everything out of the window when they were redoing the display and I felt very important in the window but we had a lady (if you could call her that) who really led me a dance. She complained about my dusting. I had to climb a ladder that leaned up against things and it did not feel very safe, in order to dust the boxes and I didn't always get to the back of them. Anyway I think the girls in the counting house upstairs saw it all and they said that they needed me up there. I gave the change through that system where the shuttle comes through a pipe driven by compressed air. I believe Valentine & Norris were one of the first to have this system. I earned 5/- and after a month a raise to 7/6 of which I got 1/- pocket money.

When I was little I used to get bundles of material for 1p for dolls clothes and so when I served on the bargain counter I used to be very generous to the kids. No wonder they went bankrupt after I had been there seven months.

I worked briefly as a cashier in the furniture department of Quin and Axton at Brixton where I was in a little box; the customer or sales staff would bring me the money for purchases. Some of the men used to tease me and sometimes prod me with a stick to get me out of the cash box.

Grace would make me dresses and I would buy myself a pair of white gloves. We would go to Clapham Common and walk around the bandstand listening to the music and show off my new dresses and almost freeze to death.

The pair of us used to go to Balham from Clapham to buy shoes from a shop near the Salvation Army called the Film Star Shoe Shop. The shoes all hung from the shelves on string and apparently had only been worn once or twice. They would cost about 5/- a pair. I had a tan pair, tan was all the rage at the time and some grey sandals. I had a friend who worked with me who suffered from curvature of the spine and was profoundly deaf, couldn't hear a word except by lip-reading. I remember she made me a dress, the material was 1/- a yard and it took four yards and it was lovely with my grey sandals

I loved colours. I once had a turquoise suit but I didn't like the jacket but I wore the skirt with a tan jacket. I don't expect that I was given these things but I loved them. I wish I felt so good these days in my clothes but I suppose that's how the young feel.

In saying that, my sister Daisy still likes new clothes and she likes to look nice to go to church.

I was 15 years old when I went to work at Max Davis (dressmakers), 15 Market Place, off Oxford Street. Max was a shy man, big with curly hair. He had a traveller (*salesman*) named Conrad and they in turn went out to dress shops to sell their creations. I used to go with them often to look after the dresses in the back of the car. I used to get very tired and would nearly fall asleep, owing to the petrol fumes, of which I knew nothing about in those days. I thought I was just being tired and I would take Yeast Vite all the time for energy.

Max's sister used to call me as soon as it was my lunchtime, for me to go to the end of Great Titchfield Street to get her rolls & butter. Her brother wouldn't let her send me in *his* time.

There was a cafe on the corner of Market Place underneath a Parceline type place called Carter Patterson and I used to go down there and get two salad rolls 2d each for my lunch. I used to have a shilling a day to spend, 4d for my fare if I got the "workmans" on the underground, Stockwell to Oxford Circus but if you were just one minute late it would cost 8d.

The other pennies were spent on a Daily Mirror, 1d (which I still take; I liked the comic strips, Jane and Belinda Blue Eyes), 1½d on a fruit bun for my breakfast. There was a Lyons near the underground and they sold real cream sponges and the girls in the shop used to buy some on their birthdays.

We used to have a box to save money for Xmas it started off as a Swear Box but then *everyone stopped swearing (* the common ones) and so we had a weather collection. 1d for rain, 2d for hail, 3d for a thunderstorm 4d etc. I don't know what it would have been for an earthquake but we used to have a few shillings each at the end of the year.

The young lady in the office also mannequinned for the dresses as well, she used to call me just before I was going home to wait for parcels that she had to pack and for me to post. So I was sometimes half an hour late going home. Mind you, I fretted over all these things but wouldn't say anything and put up with it.

I started work earning 15/- and by 1939 when the war came, I was getting 27/6. I left once to become a presser underneath the showrooms but the first thing they gave me to press was a velvet dress; well I knew I had to put the iron underneath to bring up the velvet but it was a faulty iron and it fell on my arm burning me and so

I went back to Max's and that's when I got the extra 2/6. The manageress, Miss Honor, didn't tell Max that I left for a morning. I became a finisher and matcher which involved sewing buttons on the dresses and making handmade loops for the belts and as I was the youngest, I would go shopping to match cottons to the cloths.
This matching took me to an assortment of shops; Falbers in Oxford Street, Diamonds in Margaret Street, a lace shop in Green (something) and the big stores like Bourne & Hollingsworth, Evans and John Lewis.

I continued to work there until the war broke out and Max sent a letter "not to come in until further notice". I'm still waiting.

I am 76 years of age now and I still go up to Oxford Street and make for Market Place.
Back then, on my visits to the shops to get material, ribbons and made up and artificial flowers for evening dresses and I would meet young men who asked me out. There was one in a dress material shop who I thought was nice and all the girls were after him and he asked if I could meet him on the Saturday after lunch as he enjoyed a lie in on a Saturday. I was to meet him at Willesden Green, I don't know how I found it but anyway, he took me on a bus to Wembley and a park. We walked hand in hand and then he laid out his raincoat and wanted to make love. I wasn't very pleased with this suggestion and he replied that I could get my bus over the road. I saw a bus going to Victoria and I knew the way home from there.
Afterwards, he often teased me by asking if I was still a good girl. I was about 17 then.

I had met John, a Welshman, at Sunday School when I was 15 years old and he was 20.
He had his apprenticeship in Aberystwyth and then sent to London. We became friends but I wasn't keen to go out with him until about six months after I met him, the occasion was when he was going home for the Easter holidays and he kissed my friend goodbye, turning me green. I allowed him to kiss me that afternoon. Before that we had always shook hands.

When I was sixteen, his mother invited me to go and see them. She and John's dad had a fit when they saw how young I was and immediately took him to a room to scold him and tell him how careful he had to treat me. His father also took me for a walk & told me that John wouldn't want to get married for years otherwise he would spoil his career.
I had a lovely time in Wales except for his sister who was forever tormenting me by asking me what I saw in her brother. I being a sensitive type was often in tears with her trying to pacify me with chocolates while sharing her bedroom while I stayed there.

I was so impressed by the lovely way his mother ran her home, it was so clean and she cooked us nice meals and was very kind always. When I got home to London, I was so miserable with our one room (the one left from my father).

(John asked Doris not to tell anyone back home that she was asthmatic as there was a lot of fear prevailing at that time of the dreaded T.B.)

At that time, I wasn't too happy as he didn't let me out of his sight; he was at Stockwell station when I came home from work, then he waited outside my house while I had my tea and then we would go for a walk or go the pictures, at 9d each.

Sometimes we would go to his digs in Fentiman Road at the Oval. His landlady didn't like it at first but if he wasn't with me, he wouldn't stay in to study and his mother had asked the landlady to look after him like a mother.

Mrs Lawson was the name of John's landlady. She suffered a bit from rheumatism and so John would help her with the mangling for the price of a packet of cigarettes. He didn't have much money at the time. His mother gave Mrs Lawson 30/- of which John got 5/-. (*a week?*) John sent his washing home by post and his mother sent clean clothes back - so postage must have been very cheap.
Mrs Lawson moved from the two house she owned in Fentiman Road (60 & 62 I believe) to a house opposite the Oval Cricket ground so when he visited her he could watch the cricket for nothing.

John was studying Pharmacy at a college in the Clapham Road "The South of England College of Pharmacy".

I told John that I was going to Plaistow to see an aunt on that Saturday but after the incident in Wembley Park, I went and met John from his work at Loughborough Junction and owned up.
He was so sweet and sent me a letter telling me he was glad that I had told him the truth about the visit to my aunt's and seemed to understand his possessiveness. Of course, years later when he ran his youth club, he "got his own back" flirting with all the girls and it was my turn to be jealous. Even more so.
John always wrote lots of letters even when he had seen me every day. One week he couldn't sleep and wrote lots of letters, kept them all and gave them to me all in one go. I have still got all his letters.

There were three colleges in Clapham: next to the S of E was the Westminster College and further down the road was the London College.

They used to play tricks on each other, like break in and steal their mascots. They used to have college dances and I would be invited. My sister Grace had a lot of pretty dresses passed down to her by my eldest sister, Lily. Lily worked at the Co-op printing firm at Blackfriars who dressed the girls as cigarette girls at their annual event. Lily didn't dance so she passed the dresses onto Grace afterwards.

I borrowed one for the dance, a bright red Russian type blouse and a black satin skirt. I thought I was the cat's whiskers. Another time it was a blue lace dress but while dancing with one of the students, he got his button caught on it and tore it. I was terrified to tell my sister Grace as she treasured her dresses but she was lovely about it and said it wouldn't show after she stitched it together.

John had a friend called Frank Creber who was nice and he and John would play chess. Frank married at Kennington Church and I went to take some snaps. They insisted that I went back with them for tea and cakes. I was a bit embarrassed as I wasn't dressed for a wedding. I had plimsolls on and although I had nothing, I was still a bit of a snob. The pictures came out very well and I'd love to know how Frank and his wife are doing. They moved to Ruislip and he worked, I believe, for Eli Lilley. There was more money in travelling than in a chemist shop.

Jubilee Day for King George V, I was about 17 years of age and went to Hampstead Heath with Grace & came home to find John on the doorstep waiting for me after being in Wales with his family. He had a new white Mac on and that's when I fell in love, he looked quite handsome.

My War Years

I got married to John when the war broke out, we lived with my mum, Grace had already flown the coop, in the two rooms. John had qualified and now worked in a chemist shop in Loughboro Junction.

I must tell you about the wedding. Although we met in the Methodist Church at Stockwell, we started going to the Baptist one in South L Road as John's parents were Baptist. So we asked the vicar, Dicky Bird, yes honestly, if he would marry us and he said he would. It was set up for the 24th December 1939 after Sunday School at 4 o'clock. Well this particular day it was so foggy you couldn't see a thing right in front of your eyes.
I took a tram with my brother-in-law at the top of Union Road to the church and John went on the following tram with my mum. We had arranged for a friend to give me away. He and his wife (the Potters) travelled from New Malden but they couldn't find the church because of the fog.

So my mother walked me down the aisle. The church organist, a friend, played "The Bridal March". My sister Grace had made me a fur hat and she stitched fur reveres onto my coat. John said he thought it was Olga Pulloffsky coming towards him. He told me she was a beautiful Russian spy.

Afterwards, we went back to our two rooms for tea and cakes. Grace wasn't there as she was in Annie McCall hospital having a little baby, Patricia Joan, now 3 days old.

(some 26 years later, baby David Wynne-Williams was born in the same place.)

At nine o'clock we were at Paddington waiting for the train to take us to Lampeter in mid-Wales where my new father-in-law was station master. The train was packed with soldiers and while John fell asleep, I was chatting to a Corporal Jenkins who made me laugh and gave me the book he was given when he joined up as a wedding present. I've still got it somewhere. I wonder what happened to that fun loving corporal.

We only had three days honeymoon in Wales as the Wenmoth's at the shop could only spare John for the Christmas holidays.

We (Mum, John and myself) were bombed out of our Bromfelde Road flat by a landmine. They used to come down on parachutes, two were hung either side of the plane.

The first landmine fell on a road in Wandsworth and we heard all the windows of the three storey house break. John went into the house to fetch one of our landladies and her niece to the brick shelter. He had just put the door of the shelter back on when there was a noise like an earthquake..

We came out of the shelter about an hour later to find devastation. The other landmine had dropped across the road, a very wide road and the people who had a little dairy opposite us were killed along with hundreds of other people. We knew a lot of these people who had just two weeks previously visited their children safely evacuated in Wales.

We were taken to Drewstead Road in Streatham for the night, were fed and put into cubicles to sleep the night. The ladies at one end and the men at the other. The building had been a hostel for unmarried young mothers with no-one to care for them and unwanted. These girls had been evacuated for the war.

I felt a mess, I had on a pair of John's trousers to keep me warm in the shelter. There was a room full of clothes and we were told "take your pick".

We waited all day to have a meal but in the meantime I was eating Horlicks tablets & to this day the yeasty taste makes me feel ill.

The next morning, they said that my mother could go to Devon with my sister Grace who was already there and they gave mum the train fare.   They sent me and John to Balham (Dinsmore Road) to a lady with a little boy. She hadn't got the front room bed ready so I had to sleep with her and John slept on the couch. The room was dark as she hadn't any black out at the windows and her small boy bit me. He turned out to be not quite "the ticket".

I wasn't happy with my lot and John had to go to work with the chemist, Mr Wenmoth and his wife at Loughborough Junction. I felt homeless and had no where to go. I had a few friends and I went to one or the other every day. We lived there for three months and then my mother came back as she didn't like it in Devon. I managed to get her into a school where they had put up the bombed out people. and then found, with the help of the billeting officer, this house in Ravenswood Road. I had three rooms downstairs and after the war, I moved upstairs to five rooms and Grace, my sister, had the downstairs (*flat*). At the time of writing I am still living here.

We had gone to Wales for Xmas and when we got back, there was a letter to say that our new landlady didn't like our bombed out furniture although there wasn't much of it left. The council very kindly got the belongings out of the two rooms but when I looked in the van, it was someone else's lovely belongings that was being stored in the back room of the house we had vacated.

I got them to take it all back and bring our things but a few weeks later Mrs Beeton turned up with the person who owned the stored stuff and told me that some silver was missing and so I let them in and showed them that I only had tin spoons etc.

With the meagre amount of money I had from the government, I managed to get two fireside chairs at 30/- each from Quin & Axtens at Brixton from their fire salvage sale and I also bought some new curtains and lino that Daisy bought for us; The place was looking quite nice and before they went, they congratulated me on the transformation of my bombed out furniture.

Anyway, we were happy in Ravenswood and were given a Morris shelter for the front room. A big metal top and thick iron legs & mattress & one slept underneath this.

Mum used to go to the shelter at Clapham South with Daisy and her in-laws. I couldn't go as I didn't like the smell of the damp brickwork. Also, I didn't like the thought of being so far down in the ground.

So, John and myself joined the fire brigade; we were taught by them how to put out different kinds of fires and we had our tests at Clapham fire station. I got 95 out of 100 and was quite proud to be in charge of the pump. It was good having friends around and they were always knocking in any time of day or night, wanting tea and biscuits.

Norman Benstead was our head fire guard and Miss Williams was senior fire guard. They were stationed at Manor Street Baths, Clapham and we used to visit them on a Sunday and be entertained with all their favourite records on a gramophone which got me interested in classical music. Favourites included "Dance Macabre" and The Sorcerer's Apprentice".

There were two other senior fire guards, Mr Maclan and Mr Coran, they were all so nice but I think I annoyed my husband that I wanted to visit the Baths every Sunday to be amused.

In the week, I had to work part-time on war work. My first job was at Smith Meters, Rowan Road, Streatham where I inspected trench mortars bodies but the girl next to me was rubbing them down on a linisher and it gave me nasal pharyngitis so after seven months I went to Rawlins in Bedford Hill, Balham making parts of Halifax Bomber wings.

My first job at Rawlins, I was given two spanners to tighten up screws simultaneously. I started to giggle and Bob the foreman asked "what's up?" I told him that I felt like Charlie Chaplin in "Modern Times and he laughed out loud. He shared a funny sense of humour and we got on well. When he and his wife were bombed out they came to live with us in the same house in Ravenswood.

Bob used to take the mickey out of me when I used the airgun. I had to knock in the rivets and I used to squash a few and someone had to drill them out. That someone had a reputation as a womaniser and they all laughed when I said he never complained about doing that for me. "Anything to get near a woman".

We would be up most of the night very often with fire watch duties and in the morning there would be a rush to work, still in my boiler suit with "Trailer Pump Clapham" on it plus gumboots. Bob used to make an excuse for me to walk around the factory with him as though I was a showpiece but I thought if that turns him on who am I to take that away.

The part-timers got put off when the company began manufacturing Lancaster Bombers and so I crossed the road to Taylor Matterson's. Taylor had lost a leg while motor bike & sidecar racing. Matterson was a big gentle giant and always gave me a lovely smile. The girls there didn't always behave too kindly towards me, I think it was because I was married and only had to work part-time (owing to the fact that I had no children). If you were single, you were required to work all day.

One day, as I was sitting there, a good looking man in army uniform came in. He was a Captain and he recognised me as he was the billeting officer at the time when we were looking for a flat for John, mum and me. One of the girls asked me to sweep up the place and I thought she was getting at me perhaps out of jealousy and I refused. I was sent to Coventry and no-one spoke to me.

Anyway, the war was nearly over and it didn't bother me much and Mr M still smiled at me.

After the war

I was so bored when the war was over although I still collected for the National Savings but I told John that I wanted a baby and in January that year *I had Christine; she was a lovely baby, a lovely little girl and a lovely lady as she grew up. I couldn't have wished for anything better.

After about six months, Grace, my sister and her daughter Pat came to live with us, as her husband Jack had left her. John and I managed to get the flat upstairs and this wasn't bad as I had always wanted a bathroom; downstairs the bath was in the kitchenette (or scullery) and there were five rooms so I had gone up in the world.

Grace had only had the flat a month when she met Len who came to live with her the next day. He had been caught in the war at Dunkirk and was a prisoner for five years.

Anyway, he was a drinker and wasn't always very pleasant and often gave us a hard time. Life with him downstairs proved difficult.

(makes it sound like a disease! says Christine)

Patricia left home at sixteen to get her own flat. She did very well at school, went into the Civil Service and is now a social worker looking after the interests of abused children.

Pat used to come to see her mother but Len didn't like her visiting me upstairs and we had always been very close.

Grace died a few years ago and Len, now 85 years old, is in a British Legion home in Broadstairs but my daughter and Pat have lovely times together now and really make up for lost time.

Pat has two children, Graham and Alison. We are all delighted at the moment as Alison, who married a New Zealander a couple of years ago, is coming back to England, so we are very much looking forward to that.

Alison has got herself a job at Harrods, (with Christian Dior) and looks as though she won't go back to N.Z. as she likes being home and visiting her mum and dad. They have just had a weekend together in France (March '97)

Back to the post war years, John as well as being a chemist, ran a youth club for years at Stockwell Methodist Church. The Reverend at Stockwell didn't want a youth club that the young folk never attended church. The boys and girls had put so much into the club and then someone comes along to spoil it all.
The club moved on to the Sunshine Hall, Colliers Wood where Frank Townley was the Minister and then a brief spell at Lynwood Methodist Hall until they needed the hall.
Finally we paid for the use of Bruce Hall in Franciscan Road, Tooting.

The club enjoyed table tennis matches & snooker and they also went out to the park to play putting. They also had Treasure Hunts & to this day, the boys who are grown up & middle-aged men now still go on these treasure hunts. They used to come back to our house after putting and play games like "Wembley" and card games. It was alright until they started to play for money and then it had to stop as they were spending more than they could afford.

They were a grand lot of youngsters. The girls telling me all their troubles, the boys they wanted to go out with and the upsets if they didn't like them enough.

We had great parties and everyone including Les Bradbury, Derek Wilmot, and Frank (Les 's uncle) blew up balloons etc but the party didn't really start until John arrived straight from work. He had that way where he was just such a lot of fun.
John ran youth clubs and planned treasure hunts, outings to the coast in coaches as well as working full time.

The last chemist shop that John worked in was at Caterham, Surrey; there were two pharmacists, John and Mr Rudd.

They used to go to the local park and have their sandwiches but just before Xmas Mr Rudd died suddenly and John was very disturbed about it. We had a Xmas party, the boss came on his return from Spain and Mr Rudd's wife gave John the present that Mr Rudd had wrapped for him, a book about cactus that we were both interested in.

Well, a month after that, a very cold Friday evening on 4th January, the trains were on strike and John had to wait for three buses in the bitter cold, he got home about ten o'clock, had his supper by the fire and went straight to bed. He had a heart attack in the night, just shuddered and made a noise and thinking he was dreaming, I didn't really wake up and in the morning found him dead beside me. I went downstairs and made some tea before I told my son John who was 18 at the time and then rang Geoffrey. He told me to ring the doctor and that he would come to the house.
The doctor got the coroner down and Geoffrey contacted the undertakers.

It has always seemed a bit of a dream for me as one minute John was here and the next taken out of the house.

-O-

Printed in Great Britain
by Amazon